To

Michelle & Mike

With Love

Mom & Dad

On

August, 24, 2002

JUST MARRIED

Happily Ever After

HOLLY POND HILL®
BY SUSAN WHEELER

HARVEST HOUSE PUBLISHERS
Eugene, Oregon

Happily Ever After

Text Copyright © 2002 by Harvest House Publishers
Eugene, Oregon 97402

ISBN 0-7369-0788-2

> InterArt® Licensing
> P.O. Box 4699
> Bloomington, IN 47402-4699
> 800-457-4045

Design and production by Garborg Design Works, Minneapolis, Minnesota

Scripture quotations are taken from the Holy Bible, New International Version®, Copyright © 1973, 1978, 1984 by the International Bible Society. Used by permission of Zondervan Publishing House.

Harvest House Publishers has made every effort to trace the ownership of all poems and quotes. In the event of a question arising from the use of a poem or quote, we regret any error made and will be pleased to make the necessary correction in future editions of this book.

Printed in Hong Kong

02 03 04 05 06 07 08 09 10 11/ NG / 10 9 8 7 6 5 4 3 2 1

From this day forward,

You shall not walk alone.

My heart will be your shelter,

And my arms will be your home.

AUTHOR UNKNOWN

Today I begin to understand what love is...
When we are parted, we each feel the lack of the other
half of ourselves.
We are incomplete like a book in two volumes
of which the first has been lost.
That is what I know love to be: incompleteness in absence.

ALEXANDRE HAZEN DORNBACK

Love is...

running into

his arms,

Colliding with

his heart,

And exploding

into his soul.

AUTHOR UNKNOWN

A soul mate is someone who has locks that fit our keys, and keys to fit our locks. When we feel safe enough to open the locks, our truest selves step out and we can be completely and honestly who we are; we can be loved for who we are and not for who we're pretending to be. Each unveils the best part of the other. No matter what else goes wrong around us, with that one person we're safe in our own paradise. Our soul mate is someone who shares our deepest longings, our sense of direction. When we're two balloons, and together our direction is up, chances are we've found the right person. Our soul mate is the one who makes life come to life.

RICHARD BACH

Susan
Wheeler

$\mathcal{U}$ltimately the bond of all
companionship, whether in marriage
or in friendship, is conversation.

OSCAR WILDE

No happiness

is like unto it,

no love so great

as that of man

and wife...

ROBERT BURTON

Acts 4:12

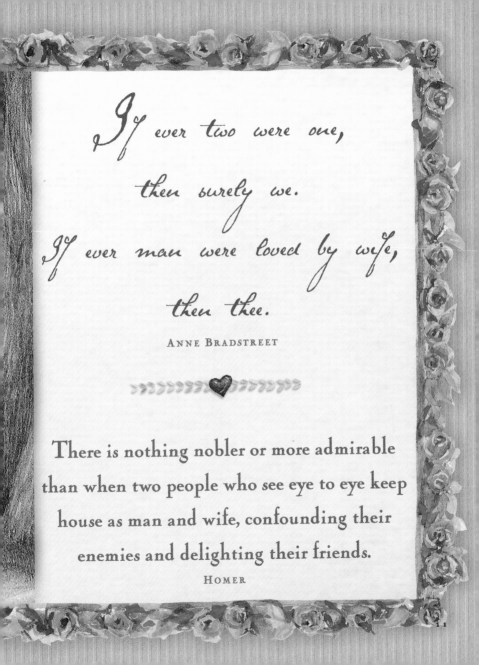

If ever two were one,

then surely we.

If ever man were loved by wife,

then thee.

ANNE BRADSTREET

There is nothing nobler or more admirable than when two people who see eye to eye keep house as man and wife, confounding their enemies and delighting their friends.

HOMER

You have lifted my very soul up into the light of your soul, and I am not ever likely to mistake it for the common daylight.

ELIZABETH BARRETT BROWNING

Two souls with but a single thought,

Two hearts that beat as one.

FREDRICH HALM

Now join your hands, and with your hands your hearts.

WILLIAM SHAKESPEARE

What greater thing is there for two human souls than to feel that they are joined together to strengthen each other in all labour, to minister to each other in all sorrow, to share with each other in all gladness, to be one with each other in the silent unspoken memories.

GEORGE ELIOT

*M*ay your marriage bring you all the exquisite excitements a marriage should bring, and may life grant you also patience, tolerance, and understanding.

May you always need one another—not so much to fill your emptiness as to help you know your fullness. A mountain needs a valley to be complete; the valley does not make the mountain less, but more; and the valley is more a valley because it has a mountain towering over it. So let it be with you and you.

May you need one another, but not out of weakness.

May you want one another, but not out of lack.

May you entice one another, but not compel one another.

May you succeed in all important ways with one another, and not fail in the little graces. May you look for things to praise, often say, "I love you!" and take no notice of small faults.

If you have quarrels that push you apart, may both of you hope to have good sense enough to take the first step back.

May you enter into the mystery which is the awareness of one another's presence—no more physical than spiritual, warm and near when you are side by side, and warm and near when you are in separate rooms or even distant cities. May you have happiness, and may you find it making one another happy. May you have love, and may you find it loving one another!

JAMES DILLET FREEMAN

$\mathcal{B}$ut it was a happy and beautiful bride who came down the old, homespun-carpeted stairs that September noon—the first bride of Green Gables, slender and arms full of roses. Gilbert, waiting for her in the hall below, looked up at her with adoring eyes. She was his at last, the evasive, long-sought Anne, won after years of patient waiting. It was to him she was coming in the sweet surrender of the bride...They belonged to each other; and, no matter what life might hold for them, it could never alter that.

Their happiness was in each other's keeping and both were unafraid.

L.M. MONTGOMERY
Anne's House of Dreams

With this Ring I thee wed,

and with all my worldly goods

I thee endow.

WEDDING VOW
Book of Common Prayer

$\mathcal{T}$he die is cast, come weal, come woe
Two lives are joined together,
For better or for worse, the link
Which naught but death can sever.
The die is cast, come grief, come joy.
Come richer, or come poorer,
If love but binds the mystic tie,
Blest is the bridal hour.

MARY WESTON FORDHAM

I cannot promise you a life of sunshine;
I cannot promise riches, wealth, or gold;
I cannot promise you an easy pathway
That leads away from change or growing old.
But I can promise all my heart's devotion;
A smile to chase away your tears of sorrow;
A love that's ever true and ever growing;
A hand to hold in yours through each tomorrow.

AUTHOR UNKNOWN

This day I married my best friend
...the one I laugh with as we share life's wondrous zest,
as we find new enjoyments and experience all that's best.
...the one I live for because the world seems brighter
as our happy times are better and our burdens feel much lighter.
...the one I love with every fiber of my soul.
We used to feel vaguely incomplete, now together we are whole.

AUTHOR UNKNOWN

When two people pledge their love and care for each other in marriage, they create a spirit unique unto themselves which binds them closer than any spoken or written words. Marriage is a promise, a potential made in the hearts of two people who love each other and takes a lifetime to fulfill.

EDMUND O'NEILL

*N*ever marry but for love; but see that thou lovest what is lovely. He that minds a body and not a soul has not the better part of that relationship, and will consequently lack the noblest comfort of a married life.

Between a man and his wife nothing ought rule but love. As love ought to bring them together, so it is the best way to keep them well together.

A husband and wife that love one another show their children that they should do so too. Others visibly lose their authority in their families by their contempt of one another, and teach their children to be unnatural by their own examples.

Let not enjoyment lessen, but augment, affection; it being the basest of passions to like when we have not, what we slight when we possess.

Here it is we ought to search out our pleasure, where the field is large and full of variety, and of an enduring nature; sickness, poverty or disgrace being not able to shake it because it is not under the moving influences of worldly contingencies.

Nothing can be more entire and without reserve; nothing more zealous, affectionate and sincere; nothing more contented than such a couple, nor greater temporal felicity than to be one of them.

WILLIAM PENN

A Wedding Cake Recipe
for a Happy Marriage

- 4 lbs. of love
- 1 lb. butter of youth
- ½ lb. of good looks
- 1 lb. sweet temper
- 1 lb. of blindness for faults
- 1 lb. of self-forgetfulness
- 1 lb. of pounded wit
- 1 lb. of good humor
- 2 tablespoons of sweet argument
- 1 pint of rippling laughter
- 1 wineglass of common sense
- 1 oz. of modesty

Put the love, good looks, and sweet temper into a well-furnished house. Beat the butter of youth to a cream, and mix well together with the blindness of faults. Stir the pounded wit and good humor into the sweet argument, then add the rippling laughter and common sense. Work the whole together until everything is well mixed, and bake gently forever.

Author Unknown

There is no more lovely,
friendly and charming
relationship, communion or
company than a good marriage.

MARTIN LUTHER

We come to love not
by finding a perfect
person, but by learning
to see an imperfect
person perfectly.

ANONYMOUS

Susan Wheeler

The institution of marriage was begun that a man and a woman might learn how to love and, in loving, know joy; that a man and a woman might learn how to share pain and loneliness and, in sharing, know strength; that a man and woman might learn how to give and, in giving, know communion. The institution of marriage was begun that a man and woman might through their joy, their strength, and their communion become creators of life itself. Marriage is a high and holy state, to be held in honor among all men and women.

KENNETH PHIFER

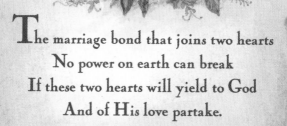

The marriage bond that joins two hearts
No power on earth can break
If these two hearts will yield to God
And of His love partake.

DENNIS J. DEHAAN

Hear the mellow wedding bells

Golden bells!

What a world of happiness their harmony foretells

Through the balmy air of night

How they ring out their delight!

EDGAR ALLAN POE

Acts 4:12

When we got into the house, all the repression of Mrs. Todd's usual manner was swept away by her flood of feeling. She took Esther's thin figure, lamb and all, to her heart and held her there, kissing her as she might have kissed a child, and then held out her hand to William and they gave each other the kiss of peace. This was so moving, so tender, so free from their usual fetters of self-consciousness, that Esther and I could not help giving each other a happy glance of comprehension. I never saw a young bride half so touching in her happiness as Esther was that day of her wedding.

SARAH ORNE JEWETT
The Country of the Pointed Firs

The story of a love is not important—
what is important is that one is capable
of love. It is perhaps the only glimpse
we are permitted of eternity.

HELEN HAYES

Love one another and
you will be happy.
It's as simple and as
difficult as that.

MICHAEL LEUNIG

All my soul
follows you, love
encircles you
and I live in
being yours.

ROBERT BROWNING

Thou art my life, my love, my heart,
The very eyes of me;
And hast command of every part
To live and die for thee.

ROBERT HERRICK

*I have found
the one whom
my soul loves.*

THE SONG OF SONGS

You soothe my soul, you fill
it with so tender a sentiment
that it is sweet to live.

JULIE DE L'ESPINASSE

Together

How happy am I, having you at my side,
Through life's ever changeable weather;
My hopes and my fears unto you I confide,
As we move heart in heart on together.
We have tasted success, we have drank of desire,
With hearts light and gay as a feather;
And the day and the deeds that our spirits inspire—
We have lived and enjoyed them together.
Through care and misfortune and trouble and pain
Made part of life's changeable weather,
And sickness and sorrow came once and again,
We met and endured them together.
So together still sharing what fate has in store,
May we go to the end of our tether;
When the good and the evil things all are shared o'er,
May we share the last sleep still together.

HUNTER MacCULLOUGH

So Jacob served seven years to get Rachel, but they seemed like only a few days to him because of his love for her.

THE BOOK OF GENESIS

The real mystery of marriage is not that husband and wife love each other so much that they can find God in each other's lives but that God loves them so much that they can discover each other more and more as living reminders of God's presence.

HENRI NOUWEN
Seeds of Hope

An archaeologist is the best husband a woman can have. The older she gets, the more interested he is in her.

AGATHA CHRISTIE

For this reason a man will leave his father
and mother and be united to his wife, and
the two will become one flesh. So they are
no longer two, but one. Therefore what God
has joined together, let man not separate.

THE BOOK OF MATTHEW

Grow old along with me,
the best is yet to be.

ROBERT BROWNING

48